EASY QUESADILLA COOKBOOK

THE EFFORTLESS CHEF SERIES

By
Chef Maggie Chow
Copyright © 2015 by Saxonberg Associates

Published by
BookSumo, a division of Saxonberg Associates
http://www.booksumo.com/

D0291354

A GIFT FROM ME TO YOU…

Send the Book!

I know you like easy cooking. But what about Japanese Sushi?

Join my private reader's club and get a copy of ***Infinite Sushi: A Complete Set of Sushi and Japanese Recipes*** by fellow BookSumo author Hashimoto Kazuma for FREE!

Send the Book!

Enjoy some of the best sushi available!

You will also receive updates about all my new books when they are free. So please show your support.

Also don't forget to like and subscribe on the social networks. I love meeting my readers. Links to all my profiles are below so please click and connect :)

Facebook

Twitter

ABOUT THE AUTHOR.

Maggie Chow is the author and creator of your favorite *Easy Cookbooks* and *The Effortless Chef Series*. Maggie is a lover of all things related to food. Maggie loves nothing more than finding new recipes, trying them out, and then making them her own, by adding or removing ingredients, tweaking cooking times, and anything to make the recipe not only taste better, but be easier to cook!

For a complete listing of all my books please see my author page at:

INTRODUCTION

Welcome to *The Effortless Chef Series*! Thank you for taking the time to download the *Easy Quesadilla Cookbook*. Come take a journey with me into the delights of easy cooking. The point of this cookbook and all my cookbooks is to exemplify the effortless nature of cooking simply.

In this book we focus on Quesadillas. You will find that even though the recipes are simple, the taste of the dishes is quite amazing.

So will you join me in an adventure of simple cooking? If the answer is yes (and I hope it is) please consult the table of contents to find the dishes you are most interested in. Once you are ready jump right in and start cooking.

— Chef Maggie Chow

TABLE OF CONTENTS

Quesadilla VII

(Chicken, Bacon, and Mushrooms)

Quesadilla VIII

(Zucchini and Carrots)

Quesadilla IX

(Sausage and Chilies)

Mozzarella, Avocado, and Olives

(Vegetarian Approved)

Quesadilla XI

(Crawfish and Peppers)

Quesadilla XII

(Monterey Corn and Beans)

Quesadilla XIII

(Cheddar and Beans)

Quesadilla XIV

(Cream Cheese and Jam)

Quesadilla XV

(BBQ Plum Tomatoes and Chicken)

Quesadilla Jalapeno Spread

Spicy Quesadilla Mayo

Squash, Mushrooms, and Peppers

(Vegetarian Approved)

Quesadilla XVII

(Casserole Style)

ANY ISSUES? CONTACT ME

If you find that something important to you is missing from this book please contact me at maggie@booksumo.com.

I will try my best to re-publish a revised copy taking your feedback into consideration and let you know when the book has been revised with you in mind.

:)

— Chef Maggie Chow

LEGAL NOTES

COMMON ABBREVIATIONS

cup(s)	C.
tablespoon	tbsp
teaspoon	tsp
ounce	oz
pound	lb

*All units used are standard American measurements

CHAPTER 1: EASY QUESADILLA RECIPES

QUESADILLA I

(CHICKEN, MONTEREY AND CHEDDAR)

Ingredients

- 1 lb skinless, boneless chicken breast, minced
- 1 (1.27 oz.) packet fajita seasoning
- 1 tbsp vegetable oil
- 2 green bell peppers, diced
- 2 red bell peppers, diced
- 1 onion, diced
- 10 (10 inch) flour tortillas
- 1 (8 oz.) package shredded Cheddar cheese
- 1 tbsp bacon bits
- 1 (8 oz.) package shredded Monterey Jack cheese

Directions

- Get a baking dish or sheet and coat it with oil or nonstick spray. Turn your broiler on to low if possible. Then set your oven to 350 degrees before doing anything else.

- Get a bowl and mix: chicken and fajita seasoning together.
- Cook contents in the broiler for about 6 mins until all pinkness is removed from the chicken.
- Get a saucepan and stir fry for 12 mins: chicken (after being broiled), onions, and red and green bell peppers.
- Layer the following on one side of each tortilla: bacon bits, cheddar, chicken, peppers, and Monterey. Then fold the tortilla to form a quesadilla. Place everything on a baking dish or sheet.
- Cook everything in the oven for 12 mins until the cheese is bubbly.
- Enjoy.

Amount per serving (20 total)

Timing Information:

Preparation	Cooking	Total Time
30 m	25 m	55 m

Nutritional Information:

Calories	244 kcal
Fat	11.3 g
Carbohydrates	21.8g
Protein	13.7 g
Cholesterol	35 mg
Sodium	504 mg

* Percent Daily Values are based on a 2,000 calorie diet.

QUESADILLA II

(CHICKEN AND ONIONS)

Ingredients

- 1 lb skinless, boneless chicken breast halves - cut into strips
- 1 tbsp vegetable oil
- 1 onion, sliced into strips
- 2 tbsps salsa
- 10 (10 inch) flour tortillas
- 2 C. shredded Cheddar-Monterey Jack cheese blend

Directions

- Coat a baking sheet with nonstick spray. Then set your oven to 350 degrees before anything else.
- Stir fry your chicken until fully done. Then combine in your onions and cook until they are see-through. Then add your salsa and shut off the heat.
- For 1 min in the microwave warm your tortillas.
- On one side of each tortilla layer it with cheese and chicken.
- Fold over the other side to form a quesadilla.

- Do this for all ingredients and tortillas.
- Place everything on the greased sheet and cook in the oven for until the cheese is bubbly.
- Enjoy.

Amount per serving (10 total)

Timing Information:

Preparation	Cooking	Total Time
20 m	7 m	27 m

Nutritional Information:

Calories	381 kcal
Fat	8.4 g
Carbohydrates	42.1g
Protein	21.7 g
Cholesterol	46 mg
Sodium	530 mg

* Percent Daily Values are based on a 2,000 calorie diet.

Quesadilla III

(Shrimp and Jalapenos)

Ingredients

- 2 tbsps vegetable oil
- 1 onion, sliced
- 1 red bell pepper, sliced
- 1 green bell pepper, sliced
- 1 tsp salt
- 1 tsp ground cumin
- 1 tsp chili powder
- 1 lb uncooked medium shrimp, peeled and deveined
- 1 jalapeno pepper, seeded and minced
- 1 lime, juiced
- 1 tsp vegetable oil, or as needed
- 6 large flour tortillas
- 3 C. shredded Mexican cheese blend, divided

Directions

- Stir fry your green and red bell peppers, and onions in 2 tbsps of veggie oil.
- Mix in: chili powder, cumin, and salt. Then add in your shrimp and cook everything for 7 mins.

Shut off the heat and add jalapenos, and lime juice.

- Heat a 2nd frying pan with one 1 tsp of veggie oil then put a tortilla in the oil.
- On one side of the tortilla put some shrimp mix and half a C. of cheese.
- Fold the other side to form a quesadilla and lightly fry for 4 mins then cook the other side for 4 mins.
- Continue for all ingredients and tortillas.
- Enjoy.

Amount per serving (6 total)

Timing Information:

Preparation	Cooking	Total Time
15 m	1 h	1 h 15 m

Nutritional Information:

Calories	753 kcal
Fat	36.9 g
Carbohydrates	67.8g
Protein	37.9 g
Cholesterol	180 mg
Sodium	1788 mg

* Percent Daily Values are based on a 2,000 calorie diet.

Quesadilla IV

(Black and Mango)

(Vegetarian Approved)

Ingredients

- 1 (15 oz.) can black beans, drained
- 1 tbsp vegetable oil
- 1/2 onion, diced
- 1 red bell pepper, diced
- 1 tsp chili powder
- 1 pinch cayenne pepper
- 1 pinch dried oregano
- 1 pinch dried basil
- 1 mango - peeled, seeded and minced
- 1 (6 oz.) package seasoned chicken-style vegetarian strips
- 6 (10 inch) flour tortillas
- 1 (8 oz.) package shredded Cheddar cheese
- 1 C. arugula leaves
- 1 (4 oz.) jar jalapeno pepper rings (optional)
- 1 (8 oz.) jar salsa

Directions

- For 5 mins heat your beans in a pan. Then mashed them with a masher or big wooden spoon.
- Lower the heat and let the beans remain warm.
- Stir fry your bell peppers and onions for 1 min in hot oil.
- Then add in: basil, chili powder, oregano, and cayenne pepper.
- Fry until everything becomes soft.
- Combine in your vegetarian chicken and mango and fry for another 3 mins.
- Get a 2nd pan and toast your tortillas for 1 min per side.
- Then on one side of each tortilla add some mango mix, cheddar, black beans, jalapenos, and arugula.
- Fold the other side to form a quesadilla.
- Heat the quesadilla in a pan until all the cheese is melted.
- Enjoy with a garnish of cold salsa.

Amount per serving (6 total)

Timing Information:

Preparation	Cooking	Total Time
10 m	20 m	30 m

Nutritional Information:

Calories	503 kcal
Fat	24.2 g
Carbohydrates	49.2g
Protein	23.2 g
Cholesterol	39 mg
Sodium	1421 mg

* Percent Daily Values are based on a 2,000 calorie diet.

Honduran Quesadillas

(Quesadilla V)

(Egg and Parmesan)

Ingredients

- 1 1/2 C. margarine
- 3 C. white sugar
- 2 C. sifted all-purpose flour
- 1 C. rice flour
- 1 tbsp baking powder
- 6 room-temperature eggs
- 2 C. lukewarm milk
- 2 C. grated Parmesan cheese
- 1/2 C. white sugar
- 1/4 C. all-purpose flour
- 1/4 C. sesame seeds

Directions

- Coat a casserole dish with oil and flour. Then set your oven to 350 degrees before doing anything else.
- Get a bowl, whisk until fluffy: 3 C. of sugar, and margarine.

- One by one add in your eggs and keep mixing. Then add: milk, 2 C. flour, baking powder, and rice flour. Mix well. Then mix in parmesan.
- Get a 2nd bowl, mix: sesame seeds, half a C. of sugar, and one fourth a C. of flour.
- Layer the first bowl into your casserole dish. Then top with the contents of the 2nd bowl.
- Cook in the oven for 50 mins. Once finished, cut up the casserole into 12 to 16 pieces. Each piece should be considered quesadilla.

Amount per serving (16 total)

Timing Information:

Preparation	Cooking	Total Time
25 m	45 m	2 h 10 m

Nutritional Information:

Calories	515 kcal
Fat	23.4 g
Carbohydrates	68g
Protein	9.9 g
Cholesterol	73 mg
Sodium	478 mg

* Percent Daily Values are based on a 2,000 calorie diet.

QUESADILLA VI

(STEAK AND ONIONS)

Ingredients

- 2 tbsps vegetable oil, divided
- 1/2 onion, sliced
- 1/2 green bell pepper, sliced
- salt to taste
- 4 flour tortillas
- 1/2 lb cooked steak, cut into 1/4-inch thick pieces
- 1 C. shredded Mexican cheese blend

Directions

- Stir fry your bell peppers and onions for 12 min in 2 tbsps of oil. Coat with some salt before putting everything in a bowl.
- Coat each of your tortillas with oil on 1 side. Then toast then in the pan on the oiled side.
- Layer half of each on your tortilla while in the pan: onion mix, steak mix, cheese mix.
- Place another tortilla on top with it, oiled side facing upwards.

- Fry this quesadilla for 5 mins per side with a low to medium heat. Place it to the side and cut it in half.
- Do the same for the other tortilla and the rest of the ingredients.
- Enjoy.

Amount per serving (4 total)

Timing Information:

Preparation	Cooking	Total Time
10 m	15 m	25 m

Nutritional Information:

Calories	552 kcal
Fat	31.1 g
Carbohydrates	40g
Protein	28 g
Cholesterol	79 mg
Sodium	859 mg

* Percent Daily Values are based on a 2,000 calorie diet.

Quesadilla VII

(Chicken, Bacon, and Mushrooms)

Ingredients

- 1 lb thinly sliced chicken breast meat
- 1/2 tsp salt
- 1/2 tsp ground black pepper
- 2 tbsps olive oil
- 14 slices precooked bacon, diced
- 1 (8 oz.) package sliced fresh mushrooms
- 1 C. Alfredo sauce
- 1 tsp butter, or more if needed
- 5 large flour tortillas
- 2 C. shredded mozzarella cheese

Directions

- Stir fry your chicken for 12 mins in oil after seasoning it with pepper and salt.
- Set aside, remove excess oils from the pan, and julienne your chicken.
- For 6 mins cook your mushrooms and bacon in the same pan. Then set the heat to low. Add in your Alfredo sauce and chicken. Cook for 3 mins.

- Get another pan and toast your tortillas in melted butter. On one side of the tortilla add 1/5 of your chicken mushroom mix. Then put 1/5 of your cheese. Fold the other side to form a quesadilla. Cook for 4 mins per side.
- Repeat for all ingredients. Once everything is done. Cut each quesadilla in half.
- Enjoy.

Amount per serving (5 total)

Timing Information:

Preparation	Cooking	Total Time
20 m	30 m	50 m

Nutritional Information:

Calories	880 kcal
Fat	46.2 g
Carbohydrates	65.6g
Protein	49.6 g
Cholesterol	121 mg
Sodium	2178 mg

* Percent Daily Values are based on a 2,000 calorie diet.

QUESADILLA VIII

(ZUCCHINI AND CARROTS)

Ingredients

- 1 zucchini, cubed
- 1 head fresh broccoli, diced
- 1 red bell pepper, diced
- 1 carrot, diced
- 1 yellow onion, diced
- 4 small button mushrooms, diced
- 4 (10 inch) flour tortillas
- 1/2 C. shredded sharp Cheddar cheese
- 1/2 C. shredded Monterey Jack cheese

Directions

- Line a baking dish or sheet with foil. Then turn on your broiler to its low setting if possible before doing anything else.
- For 8 mins with a steamer cook the following over one inch of boiling water and covered: mushrooms, zucchini, onions, broccoli, carrots, and bell peppers.
- Get your baking sheet or dish and put into it two tortillas. Layer the following: Monterey, vegetables, cheddar, and another tortilla.

- Broil the contents until the cheese is bubbly. You should try to flip the tortillas to brown both sides, but this not necessary.
- Enjoy.

Amount per serving (2 total)

Timing Information:

Preparation	Cooking	Total Time
10 m	30 m	40 m

Nutritional Information:

Calories	787 kcal
Fat	30.1 g
Carbohydrates	99.7g
Protein	33.1 g
Cholesterol	55 mg
Sodium	1309 mg

* Percent Daily Values are based on a 2,000 calorie diet.

QUESADILLA IX

(SAUSAGE AND CHILIES)

Ingredients

- 1 tbsp canola oil
- 2 andouille sausage links, finely minced
- 1 Poblano chili, finely minced
- 1/2 red bell pepper, finely minced
- 1/2 large red onion, finely minced
- 1/2 C. frozen corn kernels
- 4 flour tortillas
- 2 C. shredded Colby cheese
- 1 tbsp canola oil
- 1/4 C. sour cream (optional)
- 1/4 C. salsa (optional)

Directions

- Cook the following in 1 tbsp of canola for 16 mins: corn, sausage, red onions, Poblano and red peppers.
- Layer a fourth of the sausage mix on one side of your tortillas. Then fold the other side to make a quesadilla. Do this for all the tortillas.

- Get a 2nd pan and cook each quesadilla in 1 tbsp of canola for 4 mins per side until the cheese is bubbly.
- Once all the quesadillas have been cooked cut them in half.
- Enjoy with a dollop of salsa and sour cream.

Amount per serving (4 total)

Timing Information:

Preparation	Cooking	Total Time
15 m	25 m	40 m

Nutritional Information:

Calories	598 kcal
Fat	35.9 g
Carbohydrates	47.7g
Protein	22 g
Cholesterol	64 mg
Sodium	967 mg

* Percent Daily Values are based on a 2,000 calorie diet.

Mozzarella, Avocado, and Olives

(Vegetarian Approved)

Ingredients

- 10 (6 inch) corn tortillas
- 2 C. shredded mozzarella cheese
- 1 (2 oz.) can sliced black olives
- 2 avocados - peeled, pitted and sliced
- 2 tsps hot pepper sauce

Directions

- Toast your tortilla in a pan for 2 mins per side. Then layer one fourth of your cheese, some avocado, olives, and hot sauce. Top with another tortilla to form a quesadilla.
- Place a lid on the pan and after 1 min turn it to its opposite side. Place the quesadilla to the side and repeat.
- Cut the quesadilla in half before serving.
- Enjoy.

Amount per serving (5 total)

Timing Information:

Preparation	Cooking	Total Time
10 m	10 m	20 m

Nutritional Information:

Calories	389 kcal
Fat	24.5 g
Carbohydrates	31.8g
Protein	14.6 g
Cholesterol	35 mg
Sodium	457 mg

* Percent Daily Values are based on a 2,000 calorie diet.

QUESADILLA XI

(CRAWFISH AND PEPPERS)

Ingredients

- 1 tbsp butter
- 1 tbsp olive oil
- 1/2 red bell pepper, minced
- 4 green onions, sliced thin
- 1 tbsp fajita seasoning
- 1/2 tsp cayenne pepper
- 12 oz. cooked and peeled whole crawfish tails
- 6 (10 inch) flour tortillas
- 8 oz. crumbled queso fresco cheese
- 1 tbsp butter
- 1 tbsp olive oil

Directions

- Get a bowl, mix: onions, bell peppers, and fajita seasoning.
- Cook the mix for 5 mins in 1 tbsp of olive oil and 1 tbsp of butter. Then add your crawfish and cook for about 3 more mins.
- Layer half of your queso fresco on one side of your tortillas. Then add some crawfish mix, and

top with the rest of the cheese. Fold the tortillas in half to form a quesadilla.

- Get another pan and toast the quesadilla in 1 tbsp of olive oil and 1 tbsp of butter for 4 mins per side.
- Once finished add more butter and oil to the pan and continue with the remaining ingredients.
- Enjoy after cutting each quesadilla in half.

Amount per serving (6 total)

Timing Information:

Preparation	Cooking	Total Time
20 m	30 m	50 m

Nutritional Information:

Calories	396 kcal
Fat	17.5 g
Carbohydrates	40.1g
Protein	18.9 g
Cholesterol	82 mg
Sodium	628 mg

* Percent Daily Values are based on a 2,000 calorie diet.

QUESADILLA XII

(MONTEREY CORN AND BEANS)

Ingredients

- 2 tsps olive oil
- 3 tbsps finely diced onion
- 1 (15.5 oz.) can black beans, drained and rinsed
- 1 (10 oz.) can whole kernel corn, drained
- 1 tbsp brown sugar
- 1/4 C. salsa
- 1/4 tsp red pepper flakes
- 2 tbsps butter, divided
- 8 (8 inch) flour tortillas
- 1 1/2 C. shredded Monterey Jack cheese, divided

Directions

- Stir fry your onions for 2 mins in hot oil. Then add in: salsa, beans, red pepper flakes, sugar, and corn. Cook for 4 mins.
- Get another pan and toast your tortilla in 2 tbsps of melted butter for 1 min. Then layer it with an equal amount of beans and cheese.

Put another tortilla on top. Then flip it and let the cheese melt.

- Repeat with additional butter for all the ingredients.
- Enjoy.

Amount per serving (8 total)

Timing Information:

Preparation	Cooking	Total Time
10 m	30 m	40 m

Nutritional Information:

Calories	363 kcal
Fat	14.5 g
Carbohydrates	45.6g
Protein	13.9 g
Cholesterol	26 mg
Sodium	732 mg

* Percent Daily Values are based on a 2,000 calorie diet.

Quesadilla XIII

(Cheddar and Beans)

Ingredients

- 1 tbsp vegetable oil
- 1 onion, finely minced
- 2 cloves garlic, minced
- 1 (15 oz.) can black beans, rinsed and drained
- 1 green bell pepper, diced
- 2 tomatoes, diced
- 1/2 (10 oz.) package frozen corn
- 12 (12 inch) flour tortillas
- 1 C. shredded Cheddar cheese
- 1/4 C. vegetable oil

Directions

- Stir fry your onions, and garlic until tender in 1 tbsp of oil. Then combine in: corn, beans, tomatoes, and bell pepper.
- Divide your mix amongst 6 tortillas and top with cheese. Put another tortilla on top of the mix to form a quesadilla.
- Cook the quesadillas in one fourth of a C. of oil for 2 mins per side or until you find that the cheese is nicely melted.

- Enjoy.

Amount per serving (12 total)

Timing Information:

Preparation	Cooking	Total Time
15 m	30 m	45 m

Nutritional Information:

Calories	504 kcal
Fat	18.3 g
Carbohydrates	69.7g
Protein	14.7 g
Cholesterol	10 mg
Sodium	913 mg

* Percent Daily Values are based on a 2,000 calorie diet.

Quesadilla XIV

(Cream Cheese and Jam)

Ingredients

- 4 (8 inch) flour tortilla
- 2 tbsps softened cream cheese
- 2 tbsps strawberry jam
- 1 tbsp confectioners' sugar

Directions

- Layer the following on each tortilla: 1/2 cream cheese and jam.
- Put the tortillas on top of each other to make quesadillas.
- Fry them for 6 mins per side in a pan coated with nonstick spray.
- Garnish with some confectioner's sugar.
- Enjoy.

Amount per serving (2 total)

Timing Information:

Preparation	Cooking	Total Time
5 m	5 m	10 m

Nutritional Information:

Calories	433 kcal
Fat	12 g
Carbohydrates	71.6g
Protein	9.6 g
Cholesterol	16 mg
Sodium	511 mg

* Percent Daily Values are based on a 2,000 calorie diet.

Quesadilla XV

(BBQ Plum Tomatoes and Chicken)

Ingredients

- 4 (5 oz.) skinless, boneless chicken breast halves
- 1/2 C. barbeque sauce
- 1/3 C. diced fresh parsley
- 1/4 tsp garlic, finely minced
- 8 (9 inch) flour tortillas
- 2 small plum tomatoes, seeded and diced
- 2 C. shredded Cheddar cheese

Directions

- Set your oven to 350 degrees before doing anything else.
- Cook your chicken breast in boiling salted water until fully done. Then remove the water. Shred the chicken into pieces. Then enter it back into the pan. Combine with the chicken: garlic, bbq sauce, and parsley. Stir to evenly coat.
- Get a casserole dish and put in four tortillas. Layer an equal amount of the following on each: chicken mix, cheddar cheese, tomatoes, and another tortilla.

- Cook everything in the oven for 8 mins. Then cut them in half before serving.
- Enjoy.

Amount per serving (4 total)

Timing Information:

Preparation	Cooking	Total Time
15 m	20 m	35 m

Nutritional Information:

Calories	803 kcal
Fat	29.7 g
Carbohydrates	73.8g
Protein	57 g
Cholesterol	142 mg
Sodium	1536 mg

* Percent Daily Values are based on a 2,000 calorie diet.

Quesadilla Jalapeno Spread

Spicy Quesadilla Mayo

Maggie's Thoughts: This recipe can be used stand alone in warmed tortillas to make a simple quesadilla. But this can also be used in any quesadilla recipe to enhance the flavor. Just spread a tbsp on one of your tortillas before layering other ingredients.

Ingredients

- 1/4 C. mayonnaise
- 2 tsps minced canned jalapeno peppers
- 2 tsps juice from canned jalapeno peppers
- 1/2 tsp ground cumin
- 3/4 tsp sugar
- 1/2 tsp paprika
- 1/8 tsp cayenne pepper
- 1/8 tsp garlic powder
- dash salt

Directions

- Blend or process the following in your chosen appliance for 2 mins: garlic powder, mayo,

cayenne, minced jalapenos, paprika, sugar, jalapeno juice, and cumin.
- Before spreading over tortillas add your preferred amount of salt.
- Enjoy.

Amount per serving (6 total)

Timing Information:

Preparation	Cooking	Total Time
15 m		15 m

Nutritional Information:

Calories	70 kcal
Fat	7.4 g
Carbohydrates	1.1g
Protein	0.2 g
Cholesterol	3 mg
Sodium	149 mg

* Percent Daily Values are based on a 2,000 calorie diet.

Squash, Mushrooms, and Peppers

(Vegetarian Approved)

Ingredients

- 1/2 C. diced red bell pepper
- 1/2 C. diced zucchini
- 1/2 C. diced yellow squash
- 1/2 C. diced red onion
- 1/2 C. diced mushrooms
- 1 tbsp olive oil
- cooking spray
- 6 (9 inch) whole wheat tortillas
- 1 1/4 C. shredded reduced-fat sharp Cheddar cheese

Directions

- For 8 mins cook the following in a pan coated with nonstick spray: mushrooms, red pepper, onions, squash, and zucchini. Set aside.
- Add more spray to the pan and add in 1 tortilla. Layer the following on it: 1/8 C. cheese, 3/4 C. veggie mix, 1/4 C. cheese, and another tortilla. Repeat.
- Toast the quesadilla for 4 mins per side. Then dice it into two pieces before serving.

- Enjoy.

Amount per serving (6 total)

Timing Information:

Preparation	Cooking	Total Time
15 m	15 m	30 m

Nutritional Information:

Calories	209 kcal
Fat	7.1 g
Carbohydrates	36.8g
Protein	10.2 g
Cholesterol	13 mg
Sodium	441 mg

* Percent Daily Values are based on a 2,000 calorie diet.

QUESADILLA XVII

(CASSEROLE STYLE)

Ingredients

- cooking spray
- 1 lb ground beef
- 1/2 C. diced onion
- 1 (15 oz.) can tomato sauce
- 1 (15 oz.) can black beans, rinsed and drained
- 1 (14.5 oz.) can minced tomatoes with lime juice and cilantro (such as RO*TEL(R))
- 1 (8.75 oz.) can whole kernel sweet corn, drained
- 1 (4.5 oz.) can diced green chilies, drained
- 2 tsps chili powder
- 1 tsp ground cumin
- 1 tsp minced garlic
- 1/2 tsp dried oregano
- 1/2 tsp red pepper flakes
- 6 flour tortillas
- 2 C. shredded Cheddar cheese

Directions

- Coat a casserole dish with nonstick spray. Then set your oven to 350 degrees before doing anything else.
- Stir fry your onions and beef for 8 mins. Then remove any oil excesses. Add in: red pepper flakes, tomato sauce and minced tomatoes with lime, green chilies, chili powder, corn, oregano, beans, garlic, cilantro, and cumin.
- Let the mix simmer for 7 mins.
- Layer the following in your casserole dish: half of the beef, 3 tortillas, more beef, 1 C. cheddar, beef again, more tortillas, beef mix, and finally cheddar.
- Cook in the oven for 20 mins.
- Enjoy.

Amount per serving (8 total)

Timing Information:

Preparation	Cooking	Total Time
15 m	25 m	45 m

Nutritional Information:

Calories	493 kcal
Fat	21.2 g
Carbohydrates	50.1g
Protein	26.6 g
Cholesterol	65 mg
Sodium	1423 mg

* Percent Daily Values are based on a 2,000 calorie diet.

QUESADILLA XVIII

(BACON AND ONIONS)

Ingredients

- 2 tbsps olive oil
- 1/2 large yellow onion, sliced thin
- 6 slices bacon, minced
- 1 tbsp brown sugar
- 8 (10 inch) flour tortillas
- 1 C. spicy barbeque sauce
- 1/4 C. diced fresh cilantro
- 2 C. shredded Cheddar cheese

Directions

- Stir fry your onions for 7 mins until tender in 1 tablespoon of olive oil. Then combine in brown sugar, and bacon. Continue frying until the bacon is crispy. Take everything out of the pan.
- Layer the following on a tortilla: one fourth bbq sauce, 1 tbsp cilantro, 1/4 bacon, half of your cheddar, and 1 tortilla.
- Cook the quesadilla in a pan for 2 mins per side in 1 tsp of olive oil.
- Repeat for all ingredients. Then before serving cut the quesadillas in half.

- Enjoy.

Amount per serving (4 total)

Timing Information:

Preparation	Cooking	Total Time
15 m	20 m	35 m

Nutritional Information:

Calories	449 kcal
Fat	21.1 g
Carbohydrates	47.7g
Protein	15.5 g
Cholesterol	37 mg
Sodium	1286 mg

* Percent Daily Values are based on a 2,000 calorie diet.

Restaurant Style Quesadilla Dipping Sauce

Maggie's Thoughts: This is another recipe that can be used to enhance any quesadilla you choose to make. It can also be used as a spread inside of a quesadilla.

Ingredients

- 1 C. mayonnaise (such as Hellman's(R))
- 3 tbsps canned minced jalapeno peppers, drained (reserve juice)
- 1 tbsp white sugar
- 2 tsps paprika
- 2 tsps ground cumin
- 1/2 tsp cayenne pepper
- 1/2 tsp garlic powder
- 1/4 tsp salt

Directions

- Get a bowl, mix: salt, mayo, garlic powder, jalapenos, cayenne, 3 tbsps of pepper juice, cumin, paprika, and sugar.
- Place a lid on the bowl or some plastic wrap and chill in the fridge for 8 hours.

- Enjoy.

Amount per serving (18 total)

Timing Information:

Preparation	Cooking	Total Time
10 m		4 h 10 m

Nutritional Information:

Calories	93 kcal
Fat	9.8 g
Carbohydrates	1.5g
Protein	0.2 g
Cholesterol	5 mg
Sodium	126 mg

* Percent Daily Values are based on a 2,000 calorie diet.

Quesadilla XIX

(Mediterranean Style)

Ingredients

- 1 onion, diced
- 6 large cremini mushrooms, diced
- 2 large cloves garlic, minced
- salt and ground black pepper to taste
- 2 tbsps extra-virgin olive oil
- 2 tsps balsamic vinegar
- 1/4 C. herbed goat cheese (chevre)
- 4 tsps whipped cream cheese
- 4 flour tortillas
- 1/3 C. shredded mozzarella cheese

Directions

- Stir fry in olive oil for 7 mins: mushrooms, black pepper, onions, salt, and garlic, and balsamic vinegar.
- Get a bowl, mix: goat and cream cheese.
- Get another pan and toast a tortilla for 2 mins per side.
- Then layer the following on one side of it: one fourth cheese mix, one fourth mushrooms, one fourth mozzarella.

- Fold to form a quesadilla. Heat this for 5 mins in the pan. Then repeat for all ingredients.
- Enjoy.

Amount per serving (4 total)

Timing Information:

Preparation	Cooking	Total Time
15 m	25 m	40 m

Nutritional Information:

Calories	346 kcal
Fat	18.5 g
Carbohydrates	33.4g
Protein	11.7 g
Cholesterol	23 mg
Sodium	493 mg

* Percent Daily Values are based on a 2,000 calorie diet.

QUESADILLA XX

(HONEY BBQ CHICKEN)

Ingredients

- 2 tbsps vegetable oil, divided
- 1 onion, sliced into rings
- 1 tbsp honey
- 2 skinless, boneless chicken breast halves - cut into strips
- 1/2 C. barbeque sauce
- 1/2 C. shredded sharp Cheddar cheese
- 1/2 C. shredded Monterey Jack cheese
- 8 (10 inch) flour tortillas

Directions

- Set your oven to 350 degrees before doing anything else.
- Stir fry your onions for 5 mins in 1 tbsp of olive oil. Then add your honey and cook for 1 more min, put the onions in a bowl.
- Now add your chicken to the pan and also some more oil and cook until fully done. Add in some bbq sauce and stir everything.

- Layer the following on four tortillas: onions, Monterey, chicken, cheese, and another tortilla.
- Cook the contents in the oven for 22 mins. Before serving cut them in half.
- Enjoy.

Amount per serving (8 total)

Timing Information:

Preparation	Cooking	Total Time
20 m	15 m	35 m

Nutritional Information:

Calories	411 kcal
Fat	14.3 g
Carbohydrates	46.2g
Protein	23.2 g
Cholesterol	48 mg
Sodium	753 mg

* Percent Daily Values are based on a 2,000 calorie diet.

Quesadilla XXI

(Cinnamon and Apples)

Ingredients

- 1 1/2 tsps butter, divided
- 2 (12 inch) flour tortillas
- 6 oz. Brie cheese, rind removed and cheese thinly sliced
- 1 sweet-tart apple, such as Fugi or Gala, thinly sliced
- 1 tbsp brown sugar
- 1/4 tsp ground cinnamon

Directions

- Toast 1 tortilla in 3/4 of a tsp of butter.
- Layer some brie and apple on the tortilla then some cinnamon and sugar, top with another tortilla.
- Heat everything for 4 mins.
- Put another 3/4 of a tsp of butter on the tortilla and then turn it over and cook for 4 more mins.
- Before serving cut the tortillas in half.
- Enjoy.

Amount per serving (4 total)

Timing Information:

Preparation	Cooking	Total Time
10 m	10 m	20 m

Nutritional Information:

Calories	369 kcal
Fat	17.9 g
Carbohydrates	38.4g
Protein	13.8 g
Cholesterol	47 mg
Sodium	652 mg

* Percent Daily Values are based on a 2,000 calorie diet.

QUESADILLA XXII

(CHIPOTLE BASIL & TOMATO)

Ingredients

- 8 (8 inch) flour tortillas
- 2 C. shredded Mexican blend cheese
- 1 (10 oz.) can minced Tomatoes with Chipotle
- 8 slices bacon, cooked and crumbled
- 1/2 C. diced fresh basil
- 2 tbsps vegetable oil
- Sour cream

Directions

- One side of each tortilla layer: 1 tbsp of bacon, one fourth C. cheese, 1 tablespoon of basil, 2 tbsps of minced tomatoes.
- Fold the other side of the tortilla to form a quesadilla. Toast each quesadilla for 2 mins per side in a pan coated with nonstick spray.
- Repeat this process for all ingredients.
- Before serving cut the quesadillas in half.
- Enjoy.

Amount per serving (8 total)

Timing Information:

Preparation	Cooking	Total Time
10 m	10 m	20 m

Nutritional Information:

Calories	366 kcal
Fat	20.2 g
Carbohydrates	31.1g
Protein	14.2 g
Cholesterol	38 mg
Sodium	733 mg

* Percent Daily Values are based on a 2,000 calorie diet.

QUESADILLA XXIII

(AUTHENTIC MEXICAN)

Ingredients

- 3 green chili peppers

Pico de Gallo:

- 1 green bell pepper, halved, divided
- 2 small tomatoes, minced
- 1 small onion, divided
- 3 fresh jalapeno peppers, minced
- 2 tbsps diced fresh cilantro
- 2 tbsps tomato juice
- 1 lime, juiced
- 1 clove garlic, minced
- 1/2 tsp salt
- 1/2 tsp ground black pepper
- 1/4 tsp garlic salt

Filling:

- 3 tbsps extra-light olive oil, divided
- 2 cooked skinless, boneless chicken breast halves, minced

- 7 mushrooms, sliced
- 1 tbsp chili powder
- 1/2 tsp dried oregano
- 1 pinch garlic salt
- 1 pinch ground black pepper
- 1/3 C. red enchilada sauce, or more to taste

Quesadilla:

- 1/2 C. shredded pepper jack cheese
- 1/2 C. shredded Cheddar cheese
- 4 (10 inch) flour tortillas

Directions

- For 5 mins roast chili peppers under a preheated broiler to get the skins toasted. Once toasted place them in a resealable bag.
- After setting them aside for 10 mins remove the outside skins from the peppers. Now mince them.
- Dice half of your onions and bell peppers and then combine them with the following in a bowl: one fourth tsp of garlic salt, one half tsp pepper, tomatoes, salt, jalapenos, garlic, cilantro, lime juice, and tomato juice.
- Place a lid on the bowl and place the contents in the fridge.

- Dice the remaining peppers and onions and stir fry them for 7 mins along with mushrooms and chicken in 1 tbsp of olive oil.
- Combine with the mushrooms and chicken: some black pepper, green chilies, some salt, oregano, and chili powder.
- Cook for 1 min. Then add in some enchilada sauce.
- Layer the following on one side of each tortilla: vegetable mix, pepper jack cheese.
- Then fold it in half to form a quesadilla.
- Coat the quesadilla with 2 tbsps of olive oil and toast them in a pan for 2 mins per side.
- Before serving cut the quesadillas in half.
- Enjoy.

Amount per serving (4 total)

Timing Information:

Preparation	Cooking	Total Time
30 m	20 m	50 m

Nutritional Information:

Calories	706 kcal
Fat	35.4 g
Carbohydrates	52g
Protein	46.6 g
Cholesterol	115 mg
Sodium	1301 mg

* Percent Daily Values are based on a 2,000 calorie diet.

QUESADILLA XXIV

(STEAK AND ONIONS)

Ingredients

- 1 (1 lb) beef top sirloin, thinly sliced
- 2 small onions, sliced
- 2 green bell peppers, sliced
- 1 C. barbeque sauce (such as Bull's-Eye(R) Texas-Style Bold Barbeque Sauce)
- 8 (10 inch) flour tortillas
- 2 C. shredded Cheddar cheese

Directions

- Set your oven to 425 degrees before doing anything else.
- Stir fry your beef for 9 mins then add in your bell peppers and onions. Cook for 11 more mins. Then add bbq sauce and stir it for a bit.
- Let the contents lightly simmer for 12 mins.
- Get a casserole dish or baking sheet and layer the following on 4 tortillas: beef, cheddar, and another tortilla.
- Cook everything in the oven for 12 mins.
- Then turn over each quesadilla and cook for 6 more mins.

- Enjoy.

Amount per serving (4 total)

Timing Information:

Preparation	Cooking	Total Time
10 m	35 m	45 m

Nutritional Information:

Calories	927 kcal
Fat	36.4 g
Carbohydrates	101.3g
Protein	46.3 g
Cholesterol	108 mg
Sodium	1985 mg

* Percent Daily Values are based on a 2,000 calorie diet.

A GIFT FROM ME TO YOU…

Send the Book!

I know you like easy cooking. But what about Japanese Sushi?

Join my private reader's club and get a copy of **Infinite Sushi: A Complete Set of Sushi and Japanese Recipes** by fellow BookSumo author Hashimoto Kazuma for FREE!

Send the Book!

Enjoy some of the best sushi available!

You will also receive updates about all my new books when they are free. So please show your support.

Also don't forget to like and subscribe on the social networks. I love meeting my readers. Links to all my profiles are below so please click and connect :)

Facebook

Twitter

COME ON…
LET'S BE FRIENDS :)

I adore my readers and love connecting with them socially. Please follow the links below so we can connect on Facebook, Twitter, and Google+.

Facebook

Twitter

I also have a blog that I regularly update for my readers so check it out below.

My Blog

CAN I ASK A FAVOUR?

If you found this book interesting, or have otherwise found any benefit in it. Then may I ask that you post a review of it on Amazon? Nothing excites me more than new reviews, especially reviews which suggest new topics for writing. I do read all reviews and I always factor feedback into my newer works.

So if you are willing to take ten minutes to write what you sincerely thought about this book then please visit our Amazon page and post your opinions.

Again thank you!

INTERESTED IN OTHER EASY COOKBOOKS?

Everything is easy! Check out my Amazon Author page for more great cookbooks:

For a complete listing of all my books please see my author page at:

http://amazon.com/author/maggiechow